Java Programming

A Beginners Guide to Learning Java, Step by Step

Troy Dimes

Contents

Introduction

Java is one of the most widely used and powerful computer programming languages in existence today. Once you learn how to program in Java you can create software applications that run on servers, desktop computers, tablets, phones, Blu-ray players, and more.

Also, if you want to ensure your software behaves the same regardless of which operation system it runs on, then Java's "write once, run anywhere" philosophy is for you. Java was design to be platform independent allowing you to create applications that run on a variety of operating systems including Windows, Mac, Solaris, and Linux.

As you start off on your Java Programming journey, I'd like to send you off with a few resources. Be sure to visit http://www.linuxtrainingacademy.com/java and download a copy of the "7 Best Integrated Development Environments for the Java Programming Language."

Chapter 1: Preparing Java Development Environment

This chapter presents a brief overview about how to prepare a system for developing Java applications. Like most modern programming languages, there are a couple of ways to develop and run programs on a system. The first method is the conventional command line method where command line instructions are used to compile and run the code. The second method is developing applications via an integrated development environment or IDE. This chapter explains both of these methods and gives some details about the best IDEs for Java.

Contents

- Installing the Java Development Kit.
- Running your first program from the command line.
- Java IDEs: Downloading and Installing Eclipse
- Running your first program via Eclipse.

1- Installing Java Development Kit

Java is now officially owned by Oracle. Though there are several sources which allow you download a Java development kit, it is always better to get one from the official Oracle website. To download the latest version of Java, which as of 2015 is Java 1.8, go to this link:

http://www.oracle.com/technetwork/java/javase/downloads/

Once you are on the aforementioned page, you will see several a few different options including "JDK," "Server JRE," and "JRE." You want to download the Java Development Kit, so click on "JDK."

You will now see several versions of Java, each for a specific platform as shown in Fig 1.0. Check the Accept License Agreement radio button and select the appropriate Java version for your platform. For the sake of simplifying the explanation, I am going to select Windows x64 bit version which is located at the bottom. The yellow rectangles in Fig 1.0 correspond with the options I selected.

Java SE Development Kit 8u25		
You must accept the Oracle Binary Code License Agreement for Java SE to download this software.		
◉ Accept License Agreement ○ Decline License Agreement		

Product / File Description	File Size	Download
Linux x86	135.24 MB	⬇ jdk-8u25-linux-i586.rpm
Linux x86	154.88 MB	⬇ jdk-8u25-linux-i586.tar.gz
Linux x64	135.6 MB	⬇ jdk-8u25-linux-x64.rpm
Linux x64	153.42 MB	⬇ jdk-8u25-linux-x64.tar.gz
Mac OS X x64	209.13 MB	⬇ jdk-8u25-macosx-x64.dmg
Solaris SPARC 64-bit (SVR4 package)	137.01 MB	⬇ jdk-8u25-solaris-sparcv9.tar.Z
Solaris SPARC 64-bit	97.14 MB	⬇ jdk-8u25-solaris-sparcv9.tar.gz
Solaris x64 (SVR4 package)	137.11 MB	⬇ jdk-8u25-solaris-x64.tar.Z
Solaris x64	94.24 MB	⬇ jdk-8u25-solaris-x64.tar.gz
Windows x86	157.26 MB	⬇ jdk-8u25-windows-i586.exe
Windows x64	169.62 MB	⬇ jdk-8u25-windows-x64.exe

Fig 1.0

Download the .exe file to your local computer and run it. The Java installation wizard appears. The process to install Java is extremely user friendly and is a matter of just a few mouse clicks. Simply keep clicking the **Next** button on the installation wizard until you see the installation success message, as shown in Fig 1.1. During installation, you can change the installation path if you like, but I recommend you not mess with anything at the moment and simply keep clicking the **Next** button until the installation is complete.

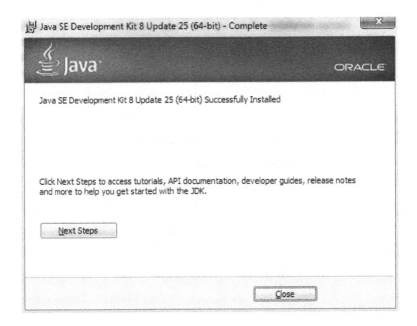

Fig 1.1

Click the **Close** button and go to the path where you installed Java. If you simply kept clicking **Next** button during installation, you should see your installation files in C:\Program Files\Java. The folder should contain two folders: jdk1.8.0_25 and jre1.8.0_25. The former contains Java Development Kit files while the later contains Java Runtime Environment. If you are installing some other version of Java, you should see different folder names. However, there will always be two folders.

Now, to see if Java has properly been installed, go to the command prompt and type "javac". You will most probably see the following output:

```
C:\>javac
'javac' is not recognized as an internal or
external command, operable program or batch file.
```

This is because the system doesn't know where to find Java. To fix this problem, right click on Computer and go to Properties > Advance Settings and then click the Environment Variables button. All the existing environment variables will appear in the dialogue. Click on New. In the Variable Name, enter Path and in the Variable Value enter the path of the bin folder of your Java Development Kit which is "C:\Program Files\Java\jdk1.8.0_25\bin" in my case. If you are using a different version of java, then this path will be different.

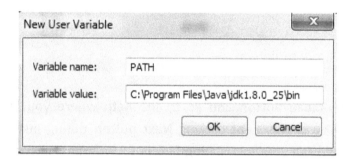

Fig 1.2

Click **Ok** and **Apply** so that changes can take effect. Close your command prompt and open it again. Now, if you type "javac" into the command prompt, you will see a large amount of output which refers to the Java version and configuration information. Here's an example.

```
C:\>javac
Usage: javac <options> <source files>
where possible options include:
```

```
  -g                         Generate all debugging info
  -g:none                    Generate no debugging info
  -g:{lines,vars,source}     Generate only some
debugging info
  -nowarn                    Generate no warnings
  -verbose                   Output messages about what
the compiler is doing
  -deprecation               Output source locations
where deprecated APIs are used
  -classpath <path>          Specify where to find user
class files and annotation processors
  -cp <path>                 Specify where to find user
class files and annotation processors
  -sourcepath <path>         Specify where to find input
source files
  -bootclasspath <path>      Override location of
bootstrap class files
  -extdirs <dirs>            Override location of
installed extensions
  -endorseddirs <dirs>       Override location of
endorsed standards path
  -proc:{none,only}          Control whether annotation
processing and/or compilation is done.
  -processor <class1>[,<class2>,<class3>...] Names of
the annotation processors to run; bypasses default
discovery process
  -processorpath <path>      Specify where to find
annotation processors
  -d <directory>             Specify where to place
generated class files
  -s <directory>             Specify where to place
generated source files
  -implicit:{none,class}     Specify whether or not to
generate class files for implicitly referenced files
  -encoding <encoding>       Specify character encoding
used by source files
```

7

```
    -source <release>          Provide source
compatibility with specified release
    -target <release>          Generate class files for
specific VM version
    -version                   Version information
    -help                      Print a synopsis of
standard options
    -Akey[=value]              Options to pass to
annotation processors
    -X                         Print a synopsis of
nonstandard options
    -J<flag>                   Pass <flag> directly to the
runtime system
    -Werror                    Terminate compilation if
warnings occur
    @<filename>                Read options and filenames
from file
```

2- Running Java Programs From the Command Prompt

Now is the time to enjoy the fruit of all the hard work you have done. Creating a basic Java program is extremely simple. Follow these steps:

- Open your notepad and type or copy paste the following piece of code in your file.

```
public class MyClass {

    public static void main(String[] args) {

            System.out.println("Have a good day");
    }
}
```

You can use any word processor; however I would recommend using Notepad++. It supports syntax highlighting and other really great features. Java source code files use the .java extension and the Java compiler considers only files that end with the ".java" extension as Java source files. Save this file as **MyClass.java**. This file naming convention is mandatory as the name needs to have the same name as the Java class it defines. In this case the name of the class is MyClass.

You have a Java source file that contains java code. However, to convert it into byte code which can then be converted into machine readable instructions, you will first have to compile this source file. To compile Java source file via the command prompt, open a command prompt and locate the directory which contains your source file, which is MyClass.java in my case. To compile this file, type the command "javac MyClass.java". This is shown here:

```
C:\>javac MyClass.java

C:\>
```

If everything goes right, you should not see any statements and the command prompt should return to the next line. Now if you go to the directory where you saved your source file, you will see another file named MyClass.class. This is the file which contains java byte code. JVM can run this file. To run your program, simply type "java MyClass" in the command prompt and you will see the output of your code.

```
C:\>java MyClass
Have a good day

C:\>
```

You can see in the output that the string "Have a good day" has been displayed. Don't worry about how this happened; we will explain that further in the upcoming chapters. The purpose of this chapter is only to show you how to run java programs.

3- Java IDEs: Installing and Running Eclipse

We saw how we can develop and run Java programs via notepad; now we will see how we can achieve the same objective in a simpler manner. IDE stands for Interactive Development Environment and it saves you from developing and running programs via command line interpreters. IDEs provide you with an extremely cool graphical user interface where you can easily develop and test your applications.

To develop Java applications, I recommend that you use NetBeans or Eclipse. Both have excellent features and capabilities and both are absolutely free. You can download NetBeans with a JDK bundle from this link:

http://www.oracle.com/technetwork/java/javase/downloads

From that downloads page, click on "NetBeans with JDK." Next click on the link associated with your current operating system name.

10

In this book, all the code snippets have been developed using Eclipse; therefore, I recommend that you use Eclipse if you want to follow along more easily.

Another reason for using Eclipse is that it is widely used for developing Android applications, so if you are planning to switch to Android development, Eclipse should be your ultimate choice.

To download eclipse, go to the following link:

http://www.eclipse.org/downloads/

You will see several versions of Eclipse there; I recommend that you download the first option, which is Eclipse IDE for Java Developers. Simply download the compressed folder and extract it on your computer. You do not need to install anything. The directory structure of the downloaded and uncompressed file will look like the one in Figure 1.3.

Name	Date modified	Type	Size
configuration	12/24/2014 10:37 ...	File folder	
dropins	9/25/2014 2:52 PM	File folder	
features	12/20/2014 6:54 PM	File folder	
p2	12/20/2014 6:44 PM	File folder	
plugins	12/20/2014 6:54 PM	File folder	
readme	9/25/2014 2:52 PM	File folder	
.eclipseproduct	8/13/2014 8:06 AM	ECLIPSEPRODUCT...	1 KB
artifacts	12/20/2014 7:04 PM	XML Document	133 KB
eclipse	9/25/2014 2:52 PM	Application	313 KB
eclipse	12/20/2014 7:06 PM	Configuration sett...	1 KB
eclipsec	9/25/2014 2:52 PM	Application	26 KB
epl-v10	9/1/2011 1:25 PM	Chrome HTML Do...	17 KB
notice	9/1/2011 1:25 PM	Chrome HTML Do...	7 KB

Fig 1.3

The uncompressed folder will contain a round, violet icon. Click this icon to start Eclipse

4- Running Your First Program Via Eclipse

Running Java programs via the command prompt is cumbersome. On the flip side, running programs via an IDE might seem like a piece of cake. To create a new Java Program follow these steps:

- Click File > New > Java Project
- The following dialog box will appear:

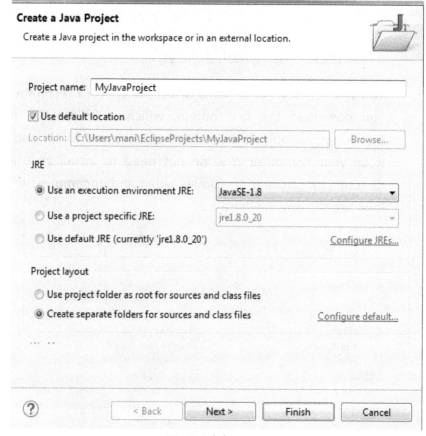

Create a Java Project

Create a Java project in the workspace or in an external location.

Project name: MyJavaProject

☑ Use default location

Location: C:\Users\mani\EclipseProjects\MyJavaProject   Browse...

JRE

◉ Use an execution environment JRE: JavaSE-1.8 ▼

○ Use a project specific JRE: jre1.8.0_20

○ Use default JRE (currently 'jre1.8.0_20')   Configure JREs...

Project layout

○ Use project folder as root for sources and class files

◉ Create separate folders for sources and class files   Configure default...

... ..

(?)   < Back   Next >   Finish   Cancel

Fig 1.4 (a)

In the Project name field, enter "MyJavaProject" and click the **Finish** button.

- The project will appear in the Project Explorer on the left panel. Right click the Project and then Click New > Class. The following dialogue box will appear:

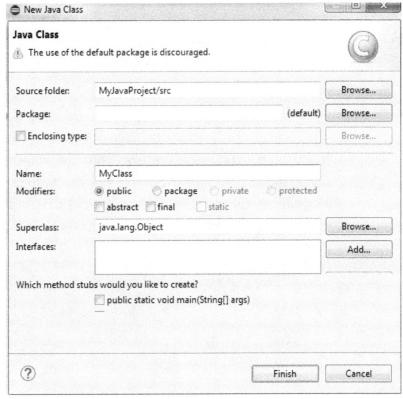

Fig 1.4 (b)

- In the Name field, enter MyClass and click the **Finish** button.
- You will see that a new file named MyClass.java appeared in the editor.

  Replace the code in that class with the following code:

```
public class MyClass {

        public static void main(String[] args) {

                System.out.println("Have a good day");
        }

}
```

- From the toolbar, click the icon with the white triangle inside the green circle. You will see the output of your program in the console window. Fig 1.5 refers to the toolbar while Fig 1.6 refers to the console window output.

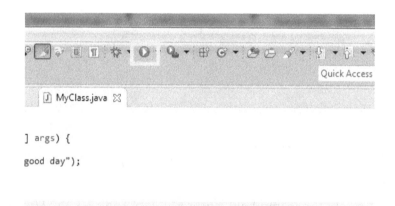

Fig 1.5

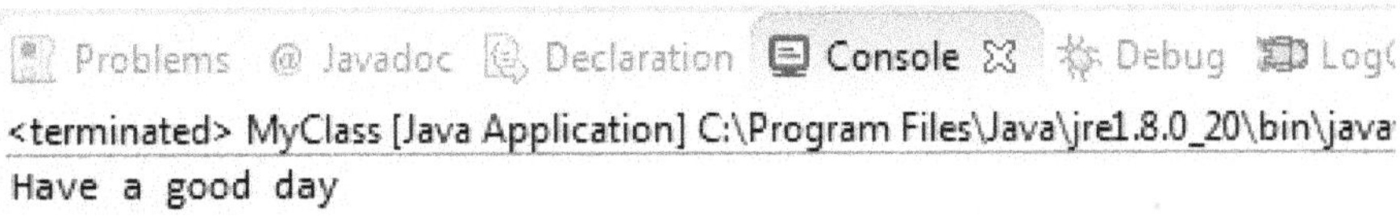
Problems
@ Javadoc
Declaration
Console
Debug
<terminated> MyClass [Java Application] C:\Program Files\Java\jre1.8.0_20\bin\java
Have a good day

Fig 1.6

Conclusion

We have come to the conclusion of the first chapter of this book where you learned how to develop and run Java programs via command line interpreters as well as through use of an IDE. In the next chapters, you will see what's happening in the code and how the string "Have a good day" is displayed in the output.

Chapter 2: Data Types and Arrays in Java

In Chapter 1, we saw how a Java program can be developed and run via the command line and an IDE. We wrote a program which displayed the string "Have a good day". In this chapter, we will discuss how that string is displayed on the console and what the flow of program execution is in Java. Then we will briefly review data types in Java, and, finally, we will conclude this chapter with the introduction of Array.

Contents

- **Basics of Program Execution in Java**
- **Data types in Java**
- **Introduction to Arrays in Java**

1- Basics of Program Execution in Java

Let's have a look at the piece of code again that prints the string "Have a good day".

```java
public class MyClass {

        public static void main(String[] args) {

                System.out.println("Have a good day");
        }

}
```

Every piece of code in Java executes within the body of a class. A class contains several methods and member variables. We will dig deeper into classes and objects in later chapters; for now, just remember that everything in Java happens within some class. To execute any program, Java runtime needs an entry point into the program. This entry point is main method. If you look at the code snippet, you will see the following line of code inside the class body:

```java
        public static void main(String[] args) {

                System.out.println("Have a good day");
        }
```

This is the function or method which executes first when your program is executed. The key word "public" refers to the access modifier of the method, which means that this method can be publicly accessed from anywhere, while "static" means that this method can be called without creating the object of the class which contains this method. When program execution starts, there is no object in the memory; therefore it is ideal to use a static method as an entry point and main method serves this purpose.

The next line prints the string on console.

```
System.out.println("Have a good day");
```

The above line refers to the println method of the "out" stream of the java.lang.System package which contains several other utility classes as well. The println method actually prints the string on the console. If you change the string inside the println method to "Welcome to my book", you will see this string displayed on the console.

2- Data types in Java

Java is a type safe language. This means that whenever an assignment or comparison occurs in Java, it is checked at compile time. A program needs to store different types of values. In Java, these values are stored in variables which belong to a specific data type. In total, there are eight data types in Java. They are byte, short, int, long, float, double, char and Boolean. These data types can be categorized into four groups:

- Integers (byte, short, int, long)
- Floating Numbers (float and double)
- Characters (char)
- Boolean (boolean)

The following table demonstrates the usage of each data type along with the range of data that each data type can store.

Data Type	Range	Width (in bits)
byte	-128 - 127	8
short	-32768 - 32767	16
int	-2147483648 - 2147483647	32
long	-9223372036854775808 To 9223372036854775807	64
float	1.4e-045 – 3.4e+038	32
double	4.9e-324 – 1.8e+308	64
boolean	True/False	Depends on Virtual Machine
char	Unicode Character set	8

Table 1.1

The following example demonstrates the usage of integer type variables:

Example 1

19

```
public class MyClass {

        public static void main(String[] args) {
                // TODO Auto-generated method stub

                byte byt = 99;
                short sht = 24513;
                int integ = 456767133;
                long lng = 1234578696;

                System.out.println("Byte:
"+byt+"\nShort: "+sht+"\nInt: "+integ+"\nLong:
"+lng);
        }

}
```

Here in Example 1, inside the main method, we have declared four variables, one for each byte, short, integer and long type. We have then stored some values in those variables using equals signs. Note that these values are in the range mentioned in Table 1.1. If you try to store the value outside the range of a particular data type, the compiler will generate an error. Then, again using System.out.println, the values stored in the data types have been displayed on the console screen. The "+" sign inside the println method is used to concatenate or join two strings. We shall see string handling in more detail in Chapter 7. The output of the code in Example 1 is as follows:

Output1:

```
Byte: 99
Short: 24513
Int: 456767133
Long: 1234578696
```

3- Introduction To Arrays in Java

If a program has to store small data, such as the age of two or three students, it is advisable to use an individual variable approach. However, if a program has to store large number of data vales that are similar in nature, using Arrays is a far better approach. Consider a scenario where you have to store the weight of ten students; you will have to create 10 integer type variables to store that data. This is cumbersome and results in a large piece of code. Arrays provide an excellent alternative. Consider Example 2 to see how Arrays would handle this scenario.

Example2:

```
public class MyClass {

        public static void main(String[] args) {
                // TODO Auto-generated method stub

                int weights [] = new int [100];
                weights[0]= 42;
                weights[1]= 23;
                weights[2]= 14;
                weights[3]= 56;
                weights[4]= 45;
                weights[5]= 36;
                weights[6]= 54;
                weights[7]= 47;
```

```
            weights[8]= 53;
            weights[9]= 28;

            System.out.println(weights[2]+"
"+weights[4]+" "+ weights[8]);

            weights [2] = 30;
            weights [4] = 45;
            weights [8] = 60;

            System.out.println(weights[2]+"
"+weights[4]+" "+ weights[8]);
        }

}
```

Closely look at the code in Example 2. Here we have created an integer type array which can store 10 integer type variables. The syntax of creating and instantiating an array is simple. To declare an array, you use following syntax:

```
type array-name [];
```

Here, type refers to the type of data which the array can store; array-name refers to name of the array, which can be anything. In Example 2, the name of the array is "weights". At this point, the array is only declared and no memory is reserved for the array variables. To instantiate an array, or, in simpler words, to create space for array variables in memory, the following syntax is used:

```
new type[size];
```

Here "new" is the keyword which used to instantiate any class, "type" is the type of data that array would store, and "size" corresponds to the number of elements that an array can store.

Back to Example 2; here we created an array named "weights" which is of the "int" type and which can store 10 integer type variables. An important point to remember here is that arrays follow a zero based indexing scheme. This means that the first element of the array would be stored at 0th index. To store and access elements in array, the following syntax is used:

```
array-name [5] = 10; // For storing integer 10 at the
5th index of the array

int num = array-name[0] // For accessing element at
0th index and storing it in integer num.
```

In Example 2, we stored 10 random integer values at 10 indexes of the "weights" array. We then displayed the value of 2, 4, and the 0th index on the console screen. Then we changed the value of these indexes and displayed their values on the console again. You will see that, in the output, the old and new values would be different which means that we successfully accessed, displayed, and updated the array indexes. The output of the code in Example 2 is as follows:

Output2:

```
14 45 53
30 45 60
```

You can see from the output that in the first line the original values stored at index 2, 4, and 8th have been displayed; in the second line, the updated values of the same indexes have been displayed.

Exercise 2

Task:

Initialize an integer type array and store 10 integers in it. Then calculate the sum of all the integers in the array and display it on console screen.

Solution

```java
public class MyClass {

        public static void main(String[] args) {
                // TODO Auto-generated method stub

                int nums [] = new int [10];
                nums[0]= 10;
                nums[1]= 12;
                nums[2]= 7;
                nums[3]= 48;
                nums[4]= 74;
                nums[5]= 13;
                nums[6]= 74;
                nums[7]= 46;
                nums[8]= 74;
                nums[9]= 16;

                int sum = 0;

                for(int i =0; i <10; i++)
                {
                        sum = sum + nums[i];
                }
                System.out.println("Sum:" + sum);


        }
}
```

25

Chapter 3: Operators in Java

This chapter gives a brief overview of the different types of operators in Java. There are four types of operators in Java. They include Arithmetic Operators, Relational Operators, Logical Operators, and Bitwise Operators. In this chapter we will briefly review the first three types.

Contents

- **Arithmetic Operators**
- **Relational Operators**
- **Logical Operators**

1- Arithmetic Operators

Arithmetic operators in Java perform the same functionality as they do in real life. These operators are used to calculate various mathematical functions. Arithmetic operators can only be applied to the operands of numeric and char data types. Table 3.1 lists these operators along with their functionality.

Operator	What they do
+	Addition and unary plus
-	Subtraction and unary minus
*	Multiplication
/	Division
%	Modulus
++	Increment a number
+=	Increment and assign
-=	Decrement and assign
*=	Multiply and assign
/=	Divide and Assign
%=	Modulus and Assign
--	Decrement a Number

Table 3.1

Have a look at the first example of this chapter to see some arithmetic operators in action.

Example 1:

```
public class MyClass {

        public static void main(String[] args) {
                // TODO Auto-generated method stub

                int num1 = 10;
                int num2 = 5;


                int sum = num1 + num2;
                int sub = num1 - num2;
                int multi = num1 * num2;
                int division = num1 / num2;
                int mod = num1 % num2;



System.out.println(
"Addition:"+sum+"\nSubtraction:"+sub+

        "\nMultiplication:"+multi+"\nDivision"+

        division+"\nModulus:"+mod);


        }
}
```

In Example 1, we have declared two integer type variables num1 and num2. These two variables store integers 10 and 5 respectively. Next, we have declared five integer type variables that store sum, minus, multiplication division and modulus of num1 and num2. Finally, these variables have been printed on the console screen using System.out.println. The output of the code in Example 1 is as follows:

Output1

```
Addition:15
Subtraction:5
Multiplication:50
Division2
Modulus:0
```

2- Relational Operators

In Java, relational operators are used for comparing and ordering two operands. Table 3.2 lists Java relational operators along with their functionalities.

Operators	What they do
==	Compare for equality
!=	Compare for inequality
>	Compare if operator on the left is greater
<	Compare if operator on the left is smaller
>=	Compare if operator on the left is greater or equal to
<=	Compare if operator on the left is smaller or equal to

Table 3.2

Example 2 demonstrates the usage of relational operators in Java.

Example 2:

```java
public class MyClass {

        public static void main(String[] args){

                int num1 = 10;
                int num2 = 20;

                if(num1==num2)
                {
                System.out.println("Num1    is    equal    to
Num2");

                }

                if (num1 != num2)
                {
                System.out.println("Num1  is  not  equal  to
Num2");

                }
                if (num1 > num2)
                {
                System.out.println("Num1   is   greater   than
Num2");

                }
                if (num1 < num2)
                {
                System.out.println("Num1   is   smaller   than
Num2");

                }
                if (num1 >= num2)
                {
```

```
                System.out.println("Num1 is greater than or
equal to Num2");
                }
                if (num1 <=num2)
                {
                System.out.println("Num1 is smaller than or
equal to Num2");
                }
        }
        }
```

In Example 2, two integer type variables num1 and num2 have been instantiated with some values; then, in order to compare them, all the relational operators have been sequentially applied to them. Do not worry if you are unable to understand the "if" statement followed by the opening and closing round brackets. We will discuss that in detail in the next chapter. The output of the code in Example 2 is as follows:

Output2

```
Num1 is not equal to Num2
Num1 is smaller than Num2
Num1 is smaller than or equal to Num2
```

Since we stored, 10 in variable num1 and 20 in variable num2, therefore three conditions became true. These three conditions have been displayed on the console output.

3- Logical Operators

Logical operators operate only on boolean operands. The result of logical operation is another boolean value. Table 3.3 lists Java logical operators:

Operator	What they do?
&	Logical AND
|	Logical OR
^	XOR (Exclusive OR)
||	Short Circuit OR
&&	Short Circuit AND
!	Unary NOT
&=	AND Followed by Assignment
|=	OR Followed by Assignment
^=	XOR Followed by Assignment
==	Equal
!=	Not Equal
?:	Ternary operator used for If then else

Exercise 3

Task:

Initialize three integers with random numbers. If the first integer is equal to second integer and both first and second integers are greater than third integer, multiply the three. Otherwise, add the three. Display the result on console.

Solution

```
public class MyClass {

        public static void main(String[] args) {
                // TODO Auto-generated method stub

                int num1 = 20;
                int num2 = 20;
                int num3 = 5;

                if( (num1 == num2) && (num1 >num3) &&
num2 > num3)
                {
                        int result = num1* num2* num3;
                        System.out.println(result);
                }
                else
                {
                        int result = num1 +num2 + num3;
                        System.out.println(result);
                }

        }
}
```

Chapter 4: Control Statements

A java program has several parts. At times, depending upon certain conditions, you may want to execute a particular piece of code while skipping the rest. For instance, consider you are developing an online movie ticketing system where you want to charge different ticket prices depending upon the age of the customer. In such scenarios, you require control statements that allow you execute a particular code segment while skipping the rest. Java provides two control statements for this purpose: the "if/else" statement and the switch statements. In this chapter, we shall see both of these control statements in action.

Contents

- **The if/else statements**

- **Switch Statements**

1- The if/else Statements

If/else statements in Java are used to execute a piece of code based on certain conditions, which results in boolean. The syntax of an if/else statement is extremely simple and is as follows:

```
If(condition==true)
{
//Statements
}
else if { condition == true }
{
//Statements
}
else{//Statments}
```

If the condition in the "if" block results is true, then the statements inside the if block are executed while the statements in the upcoming "else if" and "else" block are skipped. If the condition inside the "if" block is false, then the condition inside the next "else if" block is evaluated. If it returns true, code inside that block is executed and the remaining code blocks are skipped.

The first example of this chapter implements the movie ticketing example. Have a look at it

Example 1

```java
import java.util.Scanner;
public class MyClass {

        public static void main(String[] args){

                int age;
                Scanner in = new Scanner(System.in);
                System.out.println("Please enter your
age:");

                age = in.nextInt();

                if(age<=12 && age>0)
                {
                        System.out.println("You are a
child. Pay $12.");
                }

                else if (age> 12 && age < 20)
                {
                        System.out.println("You are a
teenager. Pay $20.");
                }
                else if (age >=20)
                {
                        System.out.println("You are an
adult. Pay $30.");
                }
                else
                {
                        System.out.println("Please
enter age greater than 0");
```

```
            }
         }
}
```

In Example 1, the user enters his age on console. This age is stored in the integer type variable named "age". Then multiple if/else statements are used to check the category in which the customer falls; depending on the category, a message containing the price of the ticket is displayed on the console. The output of the code in Example 1 is as follows:

Output1:

```
Please enter your age:
15
You are a teenager. Pay $20.
```

2- Switch Statement

In terms of functionality, a switch statement is an alternative to if/else statements. Anything you achieve via switch statements can also be achieved via an if/else statement.

If you have to do large number of comparisons, it is not advisable to use multiple if/else statements. In such scenarios, switch statements are a better alternative. Example 2 demonstrates the usage of switch statements.

Example 2

```
import java.util.Scanner;
public class MyClass {

        public static void main(String[] args){

                int number;
                Scanner in = new Scanner(System.in);
                System.out.println("Please enter your
ticket number:");
                number = in.nextInt();



                switch (number) {
                  case 15:
                        System.out.println("You won a
free burger.");
                        break;
                  case 21:
                        System.out.println("You won a
Coke.");
                        break;
                  case 24:
                        System.out.println("You won
free popcorn.");
                        break;
                  case 75:
                        System.out.println("You won a
chocolate bar.");
```

```
                break;
        default:
                System.out.println("Sorry,
you didn't win anything.");
                break;


    }
    }


}
```

In Example 2, the user enters his ticket number and, if his ticket number matches with any of the ticket numbers mentioned in each case inside the switch statement, the console displays that he has won something. However, if the number entered by the user doesn't match any of the numbers in the case statements, the code block in the default case executes, which tells the user that he hasn't won anything. The output of the code in Example 2 is as follows:

Output2:

```
Please enter your ticket number:
24
You won free popcorn.
```

From the output, it can be seen that the user entered 24 as his ticket number and the system told him that he won free popcorn. This is because the switch statement matched the number passed to it with each case statement, and then the code block inside the case statement that matches this number was executed. It is also noteworthy that every case statement has a break keyword. This is because as soon as the case is matched, the next case statements should not be executed and control should shift outside the switch statement.

Exercise 4

Task:

Initialize a character type variable. Using switch statements, check if character is equal to 'i', 'd', 'f' or 'z'. Display the name of the animal that starts with the character which matches the case.

Solution

```
public class MyClass {

        public static void main(String[] args) {
                // TODO Auto-generated method stub

                char chr = 'f';

                switch(chr)
                {
                case 'l':
```

```java
                    System.out.println ("Lion");
                    break;
        case 'd':
                    System.out.println ("Donkey");
                    break;
        case 'f':
                    System.out.println ("Fox");
                    break;
        case 'z':
                    System.out.println ("Zebra");
                    break;


        }


    }


}
```

Chapter 5: Iteration Statements

Consider a scenario where you want to repeatedly do same thing over and over again in a program. You can write hundreds of lines of code and achieve that purpose. However, in programming, there are better ways to go about this. Iteration statements provide you with the ability to execute a piece of code as many times as you want. In this chapter, we are going to look at the iteration statements in Java.

Contents

- **The "For" Loop**
- **The "While" Loop**
- **The "Do While" Loop**

1- The "For" Loop

The "for" loop is one of the most widely used iteration statements in any programing language. "For" loops are best used when you already know the number of times you want to execute a particular code segment. The first example of this chapter demonstrates the usage of "for" loops in Java.

Example 1

```java
public class MyClass {

        public static void main(String[] args) {
                // TODO Auto-generated method stub

                for(int j=1;j<=10; j++)
                {
                        System.out.println(j+" x 5 =
"+j*5);

                }

                }

}
```

In Example 1, we have used a "for" loop to display the table of five. We know that we have to print 10 statements, therefore we used a "for" loop. Inside the body of the "for" loop we initialized a variable "j" with 1 and then said to keep executing this loop until "j" becomes greater than 10. Each time the loop executes, we increment "j". This means that after 10 executions, "j" becomes 11. Since 11 is greater than 10, which is our test condition, the execution of the loop stops. The output of the code in Example 1 is as follows:

Output1:

```
1 x 5 = 5
2 x 5 = 10
3 x 5 = 15
4 x 5 = 20
5 x 5 = 25
6 x 5 = 30
7 x 5 = 35
8 x 5 = 40
9 x 5 = 45
10 x 5 = 50
```

2- The "While" Loop

A "while" loop in Java is similar to a "for" loop in functionality, with the only difference being in their termination. In a "for" loop, we already know the number of times we want to execute a code segment and we use a test condition to check if we have reached that number. For instance, in Example 1, we terminated the "for" loop after executing it ten times. On the flip side, a "while" loop terminates when a certain condition is met. We do not already know the number of iterations. We specify a condition and as soon as that condition is met, the "while" loop terminates. In

Example 2, we will again display the table of 5, but this time using a "while" loop.

Example 2

```
public class MyClass {

        public static void main(String[] args) {
            // TODO Auto-generated method stub

            int j =1;
            while(j<=10)
            {
                    System.out.println(j+" x 5 =
"+j*5);

                    j++;
            }


        }

}
```

Have a look at the body of the "while" loop in Example 2. Here, before entering the "while" loop, we have initialized variable "j" with the value. This is because if we initialized the variable inside the "while" loop, it would be reinitialized inside the body of the "while" loop. The most important line of the code in Example 2 is the expression inside the round bracket after the "while" keyword. This expression is often called a test expression or check expression. A "while" loop keeps executing until this expression returns true. It can be anything, if you simply write true in the expression body; otherwise, the loop will execute infinitely. In Example 2, our expression is j<=10 which means that we are telling the program to execute the loop until variable "j" becomes greater than 10.

Inside the "while" loop, we execute the code and then we increment "j" by 1; this is extremely important because we can only exit the loop when "j" is greater than 10. Therefore, in each iteration we increment it; when the code inside the "while" loop is executed 10 times, the variable "j" will become 11. The check expression of the "while" loop returns false and we exit the loop. The output of the code in Example 2 is as follows:

Output2

```
1 x 5 = 5
2 x 5 = 10
3 x 5 = 15
4 x 5 = 20
5 x 5 = 25
6 x 5 = 30
7 x 5 = 35
8 x 5 = 40
9 x 5 = 45
10 x 5 = 50
```

3- The "Do While" Loop

The "do while" loop is similar to the "while" loop in functionality. It also contains a test expression. The only difference between the "do while" loop and a simple "while" loop is that a "do while" loop is executed at least once. This is due to the fact that, in the case of a "do while" loop, the test expression is evaluated at the end of the loop body. To get a better understanding of the working of a "do while" loop, have a look at Example 3.

Example 3

```
public class MyClass {

        public static void main(String[] args) {
                // TODO Auto-generated method stub

                int j =1;
                do
                {
                        System.out.println(j+" x 5 =
"+j*5);

                        j++;
                }
                while(j<=10);
                }


}
```

From the code above, it can be seen that the test condition j<=10 is evaluated at the end of the body of the "do while" loop. Therefore, the body of the loop will execute at least once, no matter what. The output of Example 3 would be similar to that of Example 2.

In this chapter, we briefly reviewed three of the most basic types of iteration statements in Java. We studied the "for," "while," and "do while" loops and saw one example of each. In the next chapters, we are going to study some of the more advanced Java concepts, starting with object oriented programing.

Exercise 5

Task:

Using a "for" loop, print the factorial of 10.

Solution

```java
public class MyClass {

        public static void main(String[] args) {
                // TODO Auto-generated method stub

                int fact = 1;

                for(int i= 10; i>0; i--)
                {
                        fact = i * fact;
                        if(i !=1)
                        System.out.print(i + " x ");
                        else
                                System.out.print(i );
                }

                System.out.print(" = "+fact);
                }

}
```

Chapter 6: OOP Part 1 - Classes and Strings

In this chapter, we are going to study one of the most fascinating concepts of modern day programming, known as object oriented programming (OOP). Before the advent of OOP, procedural programming paradigm was followed where no proper code structure was maintained. Procedural programming lacked modularity and reusability. Object oriented programming was introduced to foster modularity and reusability.

Contents

- **What is OOP?**
- **Classes and Objects**
- **Constructors**

1- What is OOP?

The core idea behind object oriented programming is that a program should be divided into modules to match real world objects. An object is anything which has some properties and can perform a certain functionality. OOP states that whenever you are writing a program, you should identify potential objects and then figure out how they interact. For instance, if you are developing a point of sale system, you can identify several potential objects. A product can be considered an object since it has a name, price, and availability status. Similarly, a customer can also be modeled as an object since he or she has a name, gender, address and can perform functions like buying a product, making a transaction, etc.... Here, we have also defined an interaction or connection between two objects. A person buys an Object. Person and Object here are both objects that are interacting with each other.

Classes and Objects

In OOP, the terms "classes" and "objects" are often used interchangeably. However, these two terms are totally different. A class is similar to the map of a house. Class defines how an object will look. It defines member variables and functions that an object will contain. It has no physical existence in the memory, just as a map has no physical existence on ground. On the other hand, an object has a physical presence in the memory. Total memory occupied by an object is roughly equal to the sum of memories occupied by all the member variables. As several houses can be built using a single map, several objects can be instantiated using a single class. Example 1 of this chapter demonstrates the process of creating a class and instantiating its object.

Example1

Note: To add a new class to existing project in Eclipse, refer to Fig 1.4(a) and Fig 1.4(b) of Chapter 1.

Add a new class and name it "Person". The content of your Person class should look like the one in the following code snippet.

```java
public class Person {
        String name;
        int age;
        String gender;

        Person()
        {
                name = "James";
                age = 23;
                gender = "Male";
                System.out.println("An object of
Person class is created.");
        }
}
```

The syntax of the Person class is similar to MyClass, which we created in earlier chapters. However, Person class doesn't contain any main method since the object of this class will be created through another class and not by the runtime.

The Person class contains three variables and a constructor. We will see what a constructor is in the next section. For now, change the code in the MyClass class, which we created earlier, so that it matches the following code snippet exactly. This shows how to create an object of the Person class.

```java
public class MyClass {

        public static void main(String[] args) {
                // TODO Auto-generated method stub

                Person person = new Person();
        }

}
```

As aforementioned, the Person class did not have any main method because we said that its object would be created by another class. To create an object of any class, a keyword "new" is used followed by the constructor of the class. In the above code, we declared a new variable called "person" and then created an object of the Person class using "new Person()". Here, "Person ()" is the constructor which we defined inside the definition of the Person class. The output of Example 1 is as follows:

Output1

```
<terminated> MyClass [Java Application] C:\Program Files
An object of Person class is created.
```

As the code inside the constructor executes, the statement that we wrote inside the constructor is displayed on the screen.

2- Constructors

A constructor is a method having the same name as the class in which it is defined. Basic purpose of a constructor is to initialize member variables with some values at the time of instantiation of a class. Another important characteristic of a constructor is that it doesn't return anything, not even "void." To create an object of a class, we basically call its constructor. The code inside the constructor executes and an object of the class is returned to the calling function. If we do not define any constructor, a default constructor (not visible in code) is used by the runtime to create an object of the class.

Parameterized Constructor

There can be multiple constructors for one class. In Example 2, we shall create another constructor inside the Person class and will show you how calling different constructors of the same class result in different object initializations.

Example 2

Make the following changes in the Person class:

```
public class Person {
        String name;
        int age;
        String gender;

        Person()
        {
                name = "James";
                age = 23;
                gender = "Male";
        }

        Person (String name, int age, String gender)
        {
                this.name = name;
                this.age = age;
                this.gender = gender;

        }

}
```

In the Person class, we have added another constructor which takes three arguments. Now, when a constructor with no argument is called during object instantiation of Person class, the first constructor will execute. If the constructor is called by passing three arguments which match with the parameters in the second constructor, the second constructor would be called.

Make the following changes in the MyClass.java class:

```
public class MyClass {

        public static void main(String[] args) {
                // TODO Auto-generated method stub

                Person person = new Person();
                Person person2 = new
Person("Stacy",43, "Female" );

                System.out.println(person.name +"
"+person.age+" "+person.gender);

                System.out.println(person2.name +"
"+person2.age+" "+person2.gender);
        }

}
```

Here in MyClass, we created two objects of Person class: person and person2. The "person" object is created by calling no parameter constructor while the "person2" object is created by calling parameterized constructor.

To access the members of the object, the dot "." operator is appended with the name of the object followed by the class member. For instance, if you want to access the age of person2 object, you would write "person2.age". In Example 2, we displayed the member variables of both person and person2 objects on the console screen. You will see in the output that the person object's member variables will be initialized with values in the non-parameterized constructor, while the person2 object would have member variables as initialized by the parameterized constructor. The output of the code in Example 2 is as follows:

Output2:

```
<terminated> MyClass [Java Application] C:\Prog
James  23  Male
Stacy  43  Female
```

Exercise 6

Task:

Create a class named Car with three variables: name, price and color. Create a constructor which initializes all three member variables. Add a method which displays the price of the car. From another class, create an object of the Car class and then call the method which displays car price.

Solution

Car class:

```java
public class Car {

        String name;
        int price;
        String color;

        Car (String name, int price, String color)
        {
                this.name = name;
                this.price = price;
                this.color = color;
        }

        public void DisplayCarPrice()
        {
                System.out.println(price);
        }

}
```

Creating Car class object from MyClass.java class:

```java
public class MyClass {

        public static void main(String[] args) {
                // TODO Auto-generated method stub

                Car car = new Car("Toyota", 16000,
"Black");
                car.DisplayCarPrice();


        }
}
```

Chapter 7: OOP Part 2 - Access Modifiers and Methods

In Chapter 6, I introduced to you the fundamentals of Object Oriented Programming. We studied the basics of Classes and Objects. We also looked at constructors in detail. In this chapter, we are going to study a few other important OOP concepts. We shall start with access modifiers and their usage, and then we will take a deeper look at the methods in Java.

Contents

- **Access Modifiers**
- **Methods in Java**

1- Access Modifiers

Throughout the book, you have encountered the word "public" with the names of methods and member variables. For instance, the complete definition of the main method starts with the keyword "public". This keyword is called access modifier in Java and it defines the scope of the members of a class. They define whether a member method or variable will be accessed outside the class, within the class, or the within the package. There are three major types of access modifiers in Java.

- **Public**

Class members declared with public keywords can be accessed from anywhere using the object of the class. These members can be accessed from within the class, within the package, and also from outside the package that contains the class. They can be accessed from literally anywhere.

- **Private**

Class members declared private can only be accessed from within the class in which they are declared. They cannot be accessed outside the class body.

- **Protected**

Class members declared protected can be accessed by all the classes within the package of the class in which the member is declared. Protected members can also be accessed by the classes that inherit from the class containing the member.

It is important to note that if you don't specify the access modifier with the member variable, by default it can be accessed from anywhere within the package.

2- Methods

As mentioned earlier, anything having some characteristics and performing functions is a candidate for being modeled as an object. In Chapter 6, we created a person class which had three characteristics: name, age, and gender. We also created two constructors for the Person class. However, what if we want to calculate the bonus on the salary of a Person? What if we want to increase the salary of a Person? These are the functionalities that a Person can perform. In OOP, functionalities of any object are encapsulated via methods or functions. Have a look at the first example of this chapter. In this example, we shall implement the calculateBonus method in the Person class. This method would calculate a 10% bonus on the salary of a person. We will also add another member variable salary of type integer in the Person class. Have a look at the code:

Example 1

Create a Person class as you did in Chapter 6. Modify the code in the Person class so that it matches the following code snippet.

```java
public class Person {
        String name;
        int age;
        String gender;
        int salary;

        Person()
        {
                name = "James";
                age = 23;
                gender = "Male";
                salary = 95000;


        }

        Person (String name, int age, String gender)
        {
                this.name = name;
                this.age = age;
                this.gender = gender;
        }

        public void CalculateBonus()
        {

                int bonus = (10 * salary) / 100;
                System.out.println("10% Bonus on your
salary is equal to: "+bonus);
                }
```

```
        }
```

Person class is similar to what we have in Chapter 6; however, we have added a method called CalculateBonus and an integer type variable called "salary" in the Person class. In the constructer, we have initialized the variable "salary" with 95000. If you closely look at the declaration of the CalculateBonus method, you will see that it starts with the access modifier "public", which means that this method can be accessed from anywhere. Then there is the keyword "void" which marks the return type of the method. Void return type means that this method will not return anything. Next is the name of the method followed by empty opening and closing round brackets, which means that this method doesn't take any parameters. Inside the method, we have simply calculated 10% of the integer type variable "salary" and displayed it on the console.

In MyClass.java, the class that contains main method, make the following changes:

```
public class MyClass {

        public static void main(String[] args) {
                // TODO Auto-generated method stub
```

```
                Person person = new Person();
                person.CalculateBonus();
        }

}
```

To call a method using an object, you simply have to append the "dot" operator with the name of the object followed by the method name. In the above code snippet, we have created an object named "person" of the Person class and have then called the CalculateBonus method. The output of the code in Example 1 is as follows:

Output1:

```
10% Bonus on your salary is equal to: 9500
```

Returning Values from Methods

In the first example, the CalculateBonus method returned nothing since its return type is void. A method can also return values to the calling function. To get a value back from a method, you need to change its return type. For instance, if you want your method to return an integer value, change its return type to int. In Example 2, the CalculateBonus method returns the bonus variable to its calling function rather than displaying it on the screen. Then in the calling method of the MyJava.class, the value of the bonus variable will be displayed.

Example 2

Modify the Person class as follows:

```
public class Person {
        String name;
        int age;
        String gender;
        int salary;

        Person()
        {
                name = "James";
                age = 23;
                gender = "Male";
                salary = 95000;


        }

        Person (String name, int age, String gender)
        {
                this.name = name;
                this.age = age;
                this.gender = gender;
        }

        public int CalculateBonus()
        {
```

```
            int bonus = (10 * salary) / 100;
            return bonus;


        }


    }
```

You can see in the above code snippet that the return type of the CalculateBonus method has been changed to int. Now, to return any value from a method, the "return" keyword is used. We can see inside the method that the "bonus" variable is being returned via the "return" keyword.

Now, to access the value returned by the CalculateBonus method inside the main method of the MyClass.java, modify the MyClass.java as follows:

```
public class MyClass {

        public static void main(String[] args) {
            // TODO Auto-generated method stub

            Person person = new Person();
            int bonus = person.CalculateBonus();
            System.out.println("10% Bonus on your
salary is equal to: "+bonus);
        }

    }
```

Passing Parameters to the Method

Just as a method can return values, it can also accept values. These values are passed via parameters. The argument types that a method can accept are defined via parameters inside the opening and closing round brackets that are appended after the method's name. In the third example of this chapter, we will pass the bonus percentage to the CalculateBonus method and the method will return the amount of bonus that a person will get on his salary.

Example 3

Modify the Person class as follows:

```
public class Person {
        String name;
        int age;
        String gender;
        int salary;

        Person()
        {
                name = "James";
                age = 23;
                gender = "Male";
                salary = 95000;


        }
```

```
        Person (String name, int age, String gender)
        {
                this.name = name;
                this.age = age;
                this.gender = gender;
        }

        public int CalculateBonus(int bonus)
        {

                int calbonus = (bonus * salary) / 100;
                return calbonus;


        }

}
```

In the Person class, you can see that the CalculateBonus method now contains a variable named "bonus" of type int. This means that whenever you call the CalculateBonus method, you will have to pass an argument of type integer so that your call matches the function declaration and CalculateBonus method. Now to see how this method is called from MyClass.java, modify MyClass.java so that it looks exactly like the following code snippet.

```
public class MyClass {
```

```
        public static void main(String[] args) {
                // TODO Auto-generated method stub

                Person person = new Person();
                int bonus = person.CalculateBonus(15);
                System.out.println("10% Bonus on your
salary is equal to: "+bonus);
            }

}
```

In the above code snippet, we have called the CalculateBonus method using the person object. Notice here in the call to CalculateBonus method, we have passed an integer value "15", so now the bonus will be calculated according to this percentage. In the output, you will see that the calculated bonus will be equal to 14250, since 15% of 95000 is 14250. Here is the output of Example 3.

Output3:

```
10% Bonus on your salary is equal to: 14250
```

Exercise 7

Task:

Create a class named MathClass. Inside this class, create methods named Add, Subtract, Multiply, and Divide. Each method should accept two integer type variables. Perform the corresponding operation on the variables and return their result. Display the result of each operation in some other class.

Solution

MathClass class:

```
public class MathClass {

        public int Add(int a, int b)
        {
                return a+b;
        }

        public int Subtract(int a, int b)
        {
                return a-b;
        }

        public int Multiply(int a, int b)
        {
                return a*b;
        }

        public int Divide(int a, int b)
        {
                return a/b;
        }

}
```

Displaying results from MathClass class methods in MyClass.java class:

```java
public class MyClass {

    public static void main(String[] args) {
        // TODO Auto-generated method stub

        int result;
        MathClass mathclass = new MathClass ();

        result = mathclass.Add(15, 5);
        System.out.println (result);


        result = mathclass.Subtract (15, 5);
        System.out.println (result);


        result = mathclass.Multiply (15, 5);
        System.out.println (result);


        result = mathclass.Divide(15, 5);
        System.out.println (result);


    }
}
```

Chapter 8: OOP Part 3 - Inheritance and Polymorphism

We have covered most of the fundamental object oriented concepts. In this chapter, I will introduce you to two of most fascinating object oriented concepts: Inheritance and Polymorphism. OOP tends to imitate all the characteristics of real world objects. In the real world, objects are highly associated with each other via different types of relationships. For example, an animal has legs. Here, both animal and leg are objects and they are associated with a has-a relationship. Similarly, a car has wheels. Again, car and wheel are both objects related to each other with a has-a relationship.

An employee of some organization is a person as well. Here, employee and person are bound with Is-a relationship. A manager and a salesman are both employees. Again, manager and salesman are related to employees with an is-a relationship. In object oriented programming, inheritance is used to model is-a relationships between two or more objects. The concept of polymorphism in Java is based upon inheritance. In this chapter, we will study both inheritance and polymorphism with the help of examples.

Contents

- **Inheritance**
- **Polymorphism**

1- Inheritance

Inheritance in Java is implemented with the help of base and child classes. A base class, also known as a parent class, encapsulates those data members and functions which are common in all the child classes. Features that are intrinsic to child classes are encapsulated in child classes. This results in reusability and modularity of program. In the introduction of the chapter, we explained the relationship between an Employee and Manager and Salesman class. Try to find similarities between a Manager and Sales. Both have a name, an age, and an employee number. These characteristics can be encapsulated in their parent

Employee class. A manager has an annual bonus while a salesman has commission percentage per sale. These two properties are exclusive to manager and salesman respectively; therefore we shall encapsulate these properties in their respective classes. Have a look at the first example of Chapter 8.

Example 1

Create three classes named Employee, Manager, and Salesman. The definition of these three classes is as follows:

Employee:

```
public class Employee {

        String name;
        int age;
        int empno;

        Employee(String name, int age, int empno )
        {
                this.name = name;
                this.age = age;
                this.empno = empno;
        }

        public void DisplayName()
        {
                System.out.println("This is Employee
Class object with name:"+name);
        }
```

```
        }
```

Manager:

```java
public class Manager extends Employee {

        int annualBonus;
        Manager(String name, int age, int empno, int
annualBonus) {
                super(name, age, empno);

                this.annualBonus = annualBonus;
        }
        public void DisplayName()
        {
                System.out.println("This is Manager
Class object with name:"+name);
        }

}
```

Salesman:

```java
public class Salesman extends Employee {

        int commission;
        Salesman(String name, int age, int empno, int
commission) {
                super(name, age, empno);
                this.commission = commission;
```

```
                    // TODO Auto-generated constructor
stub
        }

        public void DisplayName()
        {
                System.out.println("This is Salesman
Class object with name:"+name);
        }

}
```

In the Employee class, we have defined three variables name, age, and empno. We used a parameterized constructor to initialize these three variables. Then we created a Manager class which inherits the Employee class. To inherit from a class, the "extends" keyword is used, followed by the name of the class which you want to inherit. Since the Manager class now inherits the Employee class, it has access to all the public and protected members of the Employee class. Have a look at the constructor of the Manager class; it takes four variables. Three of these variables have been passed to a base class constructor. The base class constructor is accessed via the "super" keyword. Three variables have been used to initialize the name, age, and empno variables of the Employee class. The fourth parameter is used to initialize the annualBonus variable, which is exclusive to the Manager class. The manager class also contains a method called DisplayName, which displays the name variable on the screen.

In the very same way, the Salesman class also contains a constructor which initializes the base class variables using the "super" keyword. It also initializes the commission variable, which is exclusive to the Salesman class.

Make the following changes in the MyClass.java which we have been using for testing purposes throughout this book.

```java
public class MyClass {

        public static void main(String[] args) {
                // TODO Auto-generated method stub
                Employee emp = new
Employee("Jacob",23, 45000);
                emp.DisplayName();

                Manager mang = new Manager ("Sara",
30, 74000, 20);
                mang.DisplayName();

                Salesman salesman = new
Salesman("Mike", 34, 84000, 10);
                salesman.DisplayName();
        }

}
```

In MyClass.java, we have created one object each for Employee, Manager, and Salesman which we have named emp, mang, and salesman, respectively. All the class members of these objects have been initialized via constructor. Note, since Employee had three data members, three arguments have been passed to its constructor. On the other hand, four variables have been passed to the objects of both Manager and Salesman class since they have to initialize three of the base class variables and one of their own variables. We called DisplayName method on each of the objects just to make sure that the objects have actually inherited the name variable from the parent class. The output of the code in Example 1 is as follows:

Output1

```
This is Employee Class object with name:Jacob
This is Manager Class object with name:Sara
This is Salesman Class object with name:Mike
```

2- Polymorphism

In Java, polymorphism is the ability of an object to perform in multiple ways depending upon the reference of the class which is stored in the object. As aforementioned, polymorphism in Java is implemented via inheritance. An important point to note here is that a base class variable can store the reference of its child classes. For instance, if you create an object of Employee class, which we created in Example 1, you can store references of both Manager class and Salesman class. However, the question that remains is how is polymorphism implemented?

If you go back to Example 1 and look at the Employee, Manager, and Salesman classes, you will find that all of them contain a method called DisplayName. When you call the DisplayName method via Employee class object, it displays a statement other than the one when you call the DisplayName method from the objects of the Manager or Salesman class. Now, if we store the references of the Manager class or the Salesman class in the Employee class object, which DisplayName method would be called? One from the base Employee class or one from the child Manager and Salesman classes? The answer to this question is the basis of polymorphism.

The answer is that the DisplayName method called by the base Employee class object would depend upon the reference which the base class object has stored in it. To have a clear understanding of what would happen, have a look at the second example of this chapter.

Example 2:

From Example 1, leave Employee, Manager, and Salesman class as they are and modify the MyClass.java as follows:

```java
public class MyClass {

        public static void main(String[] args) {
                // TODO Auto-generated method stub
                Employee emp = new
Employee("Jacob",23, 45000);
                emp.DisplayName();

                emp = new Manager ("Sara", 30, 74000,
20);
                emp.DisplayName();

                emp = new Salesman("Mike", 34, 84000,
10);
                emp.DisplayName();
        }

}
```

In the above code, we have created an object "emp" of the Employee class. We initialized the variables using constructor and the called DisplayName method on this object. This would call the DisplayName method of the Employee class. Next we have used the very same "emp" object of the Employee class to store the reference of the Manager class object. If we call the DisplayName method on the same "emp" object, the method belonging to the Manager class will be called;

finally, we store the reference of the Salesman class in the "emp" object and, this time, the DisplayName method of the Salesman class will be called. We can see that the "emp" class performed in different ways depending upon the class which it is referring to. This is polymorphism. The output of the code in Example 2 is as follows

Output:

```
This is Employee Class object with name:Jacob
This is Manager Class object with name:Sara
This is Salesman Class object with name:Mike
```

Exercise 8

Task:

Create a class named Shape. Add one member variable "name" to this class. Add a parameterized constructor which initializes the name. Add a method DisplayName which displays the variable name on the console screen with the appropriate statement. Create two classes: Circle and Square. These classes will implement their own DisplayName method. Using a test class, such as MyClass.java, show how polymorphism can be achieved in this scenario.

Solution

Shape class:

```java
public class Shape {

    String name;

    Shape (String name)
    {
        this.name = name;
    }
    public void DisplayName()
    {
        System.out.println ("This is a parent
class named: " + name);
    }
}
```

Circle Class:

```java
public class Circle extends Shape {

    Circle (String name)
    {
        super(name);
    }

    public void DisplayName()
    {
        System.out.println ("This is a child
class named: " + name);
```

```
        }

}
```

Square Class:

```
public class Square extends Shape {

        Square (String name)
        {
                super(name);
        }

        public void DisplayName()
        {
                System.out.println ("This is a child
class named: " + name);
        }

}
```

Inside MyClass.java, we will store the references of the Shape, Circle, and Square classes in Shape type object. Then we will call the Display method and see that it behaves differently. This is how polymorphism is implemented.

MyClass class:

```
public class MyClass {

        public static void main(String[] args) {
                // TODO Auto-generated method stub

                Shape shp = new Shape("Shape");
                shp.DisplayName();

                shp = new Circle("Circle");
                shp.DisplayName();

                 shp = new Square("Square");
                shp.DisplayName();


        }
}
```

Chapter 9: String Handling in Java

In Java, strings are implemented as a class and are used to store sequences of characters. Since strings are implemented as classes, they contain several functions that can be used to manipulate them. String class is probably the most widely used class in Java. You need strings in almost every program.

Note: In this chapter, whenever I use string with a small "s" I will be referring to strings in general, and when I use String with a capital "S", I am referring to the String class.

String is the only Java class that can be initialized without the "new" keyword. In this chapter, we are going to take a brief look at some of the most widely used functions that can be used to manipulate strings. We will jump straight to our first example and see some ways we can tweak and manipulate strings in Java. Have a look at our first example.

Example 1:

```java
public class MyClass {

        public static void main(String[] args) {
                // TODO Auto-generated method stub

                String str1 = "You are Welcome. ";
                String str2 = "What would you like for
dinner? ";

                //1- String Concatenation
                String result = str1.concat(str2);
                System.out.println("1-:"+result);

                //2- Getting Substring
                result = str1.substring(2);
                System.out.println("2-:"+result);

                //3- Replacing string characters
                result = str1.replace('e', 'v');
                System.out.println("3-:"+result);

                //4- Convert String to lower case
                result = str1.toLowerCase();
                System.out.println("4-:"+result);

                //5- Convert String to upper case
```

```
            result = str1.toUpperCase();
            System.out.println("5-:"+result);

            //6- Get character at particular index
            char res = str1.charAt(2);
            System.out.println("6-:"+res);

            //7- Get index of first occurrence of
character in string
            int res1 = str1.indexOf('e');
            System.out.println("7-:"+res1);

            //8-   Check   if   string   contains
particular sequence
            boolean res2 = str1.contains("x");
            System.out.println("8-:"+res2);

            //9- Checks if a string is empty
            res2 = str1.isEmpty();
            System.out.println("9-:"+res2);

            //10-  Calculate  the  length  of  the
String
            res1 = str1.length();
            System.out.println("10-:"+res1);


        }

}
```

In Example 1, we have demonstrated the functionality of ten of the most widely used string functions. A brief overview of these functions has been presented below:

- **Concat**

This function is used to concatenate the string passed in the parameter with the string on which concat function is called.

- **Substring**

This function is used to get substring from string starting from the character located at the index which is passed as a parameter to the substring function.

- **Replace**

The replace method is used to replace the character passed as first with the character passed at second index in the string on which the replace method is called.

- **TolowerCase**

The toLowerCase method is used to convert all the characters of the string to lower case.

- **ToUpperCase**

The toUpperCase method converts all the characters of string to upper case.

- **CharAt**

This method returns the character located at the index which passed as parameter to the charAt function.

- **IndexOf**

The indexOf method returns the index of first occurrence of the character which is passed as a parameter to the method.

- **Contains**

The contains method returns true of it finds the string passed to it as a parameter, in the string on which the contains method is called.

- **IsEmpty**

The isEmpty method returns true of the string on which this method is called contains no characters and is empty.

- **Length**

The length method returns total number of characters plus empty spaces in the string.

The output of the code in Example1 is as follows:

Output:

```
1-:You are Welcome. What would you like for dinner?
2-:u are Welcome.
3-:You arv Wvlcomv.
4-:you are welcome.
5-:YOU ARE WELCOME.
6-:u
```

```
7-:6
8-:false
9-:false
10-:17
```

Exercise 9

Task:

Initialize a string called "global warming". Perform the following task on this string.

- Find the length of the string.
- Join it with another string, "is dangerous".
- Find the character at 6th index of the new string.
- Convert string to uppercase.
- Replace all the 'o's in the string with 'l's.
- Print the end result on the console screen.

Solution

```
public class MyClass {

        public static void main(String[] args) {
                // TODO Auto-generated method stub

                String str = "global warming ";
                str = str.concat("is dangerous");
                System.out.println("Char at 6th index
is:"+str.charAt(6));
                str = str.toUpperCase();
                str = str.replace('O', 'I');
                System.out.println("Resultant
String:"+str);


        }

}
```

Chapter 10: Exception Handling in Java

There is hardly any piece of code with a zero bug count. A program can have a variety of errors. In Java, errors are broadly classified into two categories: Compile time errors and Runtime errors (aka Exceptions). Compile time errors are the errors that the compiler catches while compiling your program. Typical examples of compile time errors include missing semicolons or invalid type assignments. On the other hand, runtime errors, or exceptions, are those errors that are not caught at the runtime; the compiler compiles the program even if these errors are there. For instance, if in your program you are dividing a number by zero, the compiler would still compile your code, but, during execution, the program would crash giving an error that the exception was unhandled. To develop a robust program, you need to take care of compile time as well as runtime exceptions. To understand how exception handling is implemented in Java, have a look at the following example:

Example 1:

```
public class MyClass {

        public static void main(String[] args) {
                // TODO Auto-generated method stub

                int num1 = 20;
                int num2= 0;

                try
                {
                        int result = num1/num2;
                        System.out.println(result);


                }
                catch (Exception e)
                {
                        System.out.println("The
denominator cannot be zero.");
                }


        }

}
```

Here we have two integer-type variables named num1 and num2. We have initialized them to 20 and 0. We then divide num1 by num2. However, since the compiler knows that, in arithmetic, division by zero is not allowed, it will throw an exception. However, we have surrounded this piece of code with "try" block. Try block tells the runtime that if the code within the block throws an exception, the program should not crash. Rather, runtime should look for a corresponding "catch" block. A catch block is the block which is executed if an exception occurs in the code inside the "try" block. There should be at least one catch block for every try block. You can also have more than one catch blocks for a try block. The output of the code in Example 1 is as follows:

Output:

```
The denominator cannot be zero.
```

After a try and catch block, you can also use a "finally" block. A finally block always executes whether the program throws an exception or not. Finally blocks are used to clear up any memory occupied by the program and other similar stuff. Example 2 demonstrates the usage of a finally program.

Example 2:

```java
public class MyClass {

        public static void main(String[] args) {
                // TODO Auto-generated method stub

                int num1 = 20;
                int num2= 0;

                try
                {
                        int result = num1/num2;
                        System.out.println(result);

                }
                catch (Exception e)
                {
                        System.out.println("The
denominator cannot be zero.");
                }
                finally
                {
                        System.out.println("Thank    you
for using this program.");
                }

        }

}
```

The output of Example 2 would be similar to Example 1; however, in Example 2, the statement inside the finally block will also be printed on the console. The output will look like this:

Output:

```
The denominator cannot be zero.
```

Exercise 10

Task:

Initialize an integer type array with size 5. Try to assign a value at the 6th index of the array. See if an exception occurs. If it does, handle the exception. Print the appropriate message on console screen.

Solution

```java
public class MyClass {

        public static void main(String[] args) {
                // TODO Auto-generated method stub

                try
                {
                int nums [] = new int [5];
                nums[6] = 10;
                }
                catch (Exception e)
                {
                        System.out.println("You    cannot
access out of bound array index.");
                }

        }

}
```

Other Books by the Author

JavaScript: A Guide to Learning the JavaScript Programming Language
http://www.linuxtrainingacademy.com/javascript

JavaScript is a dynamic computer programming language that is commonly used in web browsers to control the behavior of web pages and interact with users. It allows for asynchronous communication and can update parts of a web page or even replace the entire content of a web page. You'll see JavaScript being used to display date and time information, perform animations on a web site, validate form input, suggest results as a user types into a search box, and more.

C# Programming for Beginners
http://www.linuxtrainingacademy.com/c-sharp

C# is a simple and general-purpose object-oriented programming language. Combine this with its versatility and huge standard library it's easy to see why it's such a popular and well-respected programming language.

When you learn how to program in C# you will be able to develop web based applications or graphical desktop applications. One of the best things about C# is that it's easy to learn... especially with this book.

PHP
http://www.linuxtrainingacademy.com/php-book

PHP is one of the most widely used open source, server side programming languages. If you are interested in getting started with programming and want to get some basic knowledge of the language, then this book is for you! Popular websites such as Facebook and Yahoo are powered by PHP. It is, in a sense, the language of the web.

The book covers core PHP concepts, starting from the basics and moving into advanced object oriented PHP. It explains and demonstrates everything along the way. You'll be sure to be programming in PHP in no time.

Scrum Essentials: Agile Software Development and Agile Project Management for Project Managers, Scrum Masters, Product Owners, and Stakeholders

http://www.linuxtrainingacademy.com/scrum-book

You have a limited amount of time to create software, especially when you're given a deadline, self-imposed or not. You'll want to make sure that the software you build is at least decent but more importantly, on time. How do you balance quality with time? This book dives into these very important topics and more.

Additional Resources

7 Best Integrated Development Environments for the Java Programming Language.
Be sure to visit http://www.linuxtrainingacademy.com/java and download a copy of the "7 Best Integrated Development Environments for the Java Programming Language."

Programming Java For Beginners
http://www.linuxtrainingacademy.com/programming-java

This video training course will help you build a strong foundation in Java and object-oriented programming with this tutorial for beginners. You'll learn about Java Development Kit Installation, Types and Operators, Object-Oriented Programming (OOP), Classes, and Objects, and Loops and Conditionals.

Projects in Java

http://www.linuxtrainingacademy.com/projects-in-java

Put your java skills to use by working on real-world projects in this video training course.

Create Your Own Programming Language

http://linuxtrainingacademy.com/create-your-own-language

A System To Achieve Every Programmer's Dream. Learn How To Create A Simple Programming Language In A Few Days With This Easy Step-by-step Guide

Java: A Beginner's Guide

http://www.linuxtrainingacademy.com/java-beginners

This book starts with the basics, such as how to create, compile, and run a Java program. Then it moves on to the keywords, syntax, and constructs that form the core of the Java language. This resource also covers some of Java's more advanced features, including multithreaded programming, generics, and Swing. An introduction to JavaFX, Java's newest GUI, concludes this step-by-step tutorial.

www.ingramcontent.com/pod-product-compliance
Lightning Source LLC
Chambersburg PA
CBHW071006050326
40689CB00014B/3505